Lines Continue Forever

Also by John Egan and published by Ginninderra Press
Reworkings (Pocket Poets)
Reworkings 2 (Pocket Poets)

John Egan

Lines Continue Forever

For my wife Marilyn, who makes everything possible

Lines Continue Forever
ISBN 978 1 74027 875 1
Copyright © text John Egan 2014

First published 2014
Reprinted 2015

Ginninderra Press
PO Box 3461 Port Adelaide SA 5015
www.ginninderrapress.com.au

Contents

For Beryl Egan	7
The wolves	8
Married in black	9
Postcard	10
Gosford Hospital	11
One White Cross	12
6th August	14
The wind	16
Jacarandas in spring	18
Sunrise: Ile de la Cité	19
The Rats	20
Goold Street	21
Rain at midnight	23
Newcastle	24
Burn	25
The Pit, the Labyrinth, the Tower	27
Commonwealth Street	29
Mosman Bay	31
From the window	33
Contentment	34
On Lines by Wallace Stevens	36
Sunset	37
Acting	38
Acting the part	39
The Spider	40
On the road, Grenfell to Forbes	41
Change of seasons	42
Discipline and beauty	44
Frog Hollow	46
Paddington Reservoir	47

Venus	48
The rain and mud	49
Closest to rain	50
An old river	51
Wind	52
Silence	53
Felling the banksia	54
At dusk	56
And yet	57
Every train	58
Unveiled	59
Bombo	60
Baby, can you hear me?	62
Erotic Poems	63
Andromeda	64
Nowra, evening	65
A black dress	66
Here to far	67
Again and again	68
Signals	69
Don't frighten me	71
Knocking	72
The transaction	73
Delphi	74
The magic city	76
Opening night	77
When your email came	79

For Beryl Egan

24/12/21–6/6/13

In the hospital
you took one teaspoon
of food, no more
and later when we thought
you might like something else
and got the nurse,
nothing.

When my brother suggested
he and I
go to the hospital canteen
for a snack
you asked brightly,
'And where are we going for lunch?'
By then you couldn't walk.

When we told you,
'Mum, today you're ninety-one,'
you said, 'Oh,
that's terrible.'

In the margin
where yesterday throws its shadow
onto this morning
you passed through
life's loophole
into the anonymity
of forever.

The wolves

There are days
when the words are forgotten
but the voice
is still heard

and evenings
after the wounds have healed
when the pain
recurs.

There are nights
when the wolves are silent
and only the moon
howls.

Married in black

Mist and rain, rain and mist.
Cloud envelops the valley
and the tall trees bury their heads
into the pillows of the sky.

In a pool of white
the escarpment presses its face
against the cliffs of cloud
like a dark woman lying prone

on a bed, her hair tossed
across white cushions, who's weeping
as the black trees sag towards her
and the rain drips from their leaves.

Postcard

Naked in the black and white
a dancer leans against
the three grim women whose
features show
they have a job to do
and shuffle forward
into time.

Clotho spins the cord of life.
The dancer bends and writhes.

Lachesis portions out the years
and then she measures hours
and minutes, then
the dancer moves no more.

Atropos holds the bloody shears
to cut the cord
that holds the theatre curtain
so it falls.

The dancer's held there
helpless in the dance –
four women intertwined
in birth and life and death.

Before the black-robed, blank-faced
goddesses of time
the dancer's naked,
then she's dead.

Gosford Hospital

These corridors, these rooms, these lifts
and the view outside the windows
have grown more familiar
over the years.

I've visited my father here
several times, once at two a.m.
when he almost died,
my mother in her late middle age
and again and often after.

I sit beside my brother now,
his arms cocooned in bandages.
He's eight years younger than me
and should in time be whole and healed.

I remember the appalling nights
I've spent in other hospitals,
once in pain so severe
I couldn't think for days. I know

that even visitors coming here,
as Philip Larkin says, are just
crude facets of the only coin
this place accepts.

One White Cross

for Marie Samueljan 1946–1994

I didn't forget the trees
on the edge of chequerboard rows,
black cement, black crosses,
plaques to mark the graves for the living
who will soon be dead,
names engraved for those who search.

Seventeen years ago I stood here
while they buried you,
the sad rituals of the Catholic Church.
Five months later I couldn't find your grave,
still unmarked.

I fled, numb with shock.

I walk the endless rows of plaques
towards the trees. Two images,
one fixed years ago,
the other flung across my eyes.
They move towards each other.
When I find you and dry my eyes,
they coalesce to where I stand
and weep, where seventeen years ago
I couldn't weep.

You died at forty-eight.
We all die too soon.

I read your name on the lifeless plaque
and see your grave for the first time –
a tube for flowers, full of dirt and grass,
no one's tended it for years.
There are flowers now,
my gift far too late.

Draw a line from the trees
towards one, white, defiant cross
which intersects your grave
and then it stops,
as your life stopped.

Geometers tell us
lines continue forever.
I hope for you
there's another
which goes on forever,
I hope it's there,
I really do,
though I doubt somehow
that's true.

6th August

Today I'll learn
to divide by twelve,
sings a schoolboy running.

Today I'll smile
at the new boy in class.
I like the way he looks,
giggles a high school girl.

I'll write
to my husband again
I haven't seen
for two years,
the young wife frowns.
He's in the army.
They say
the war's going badly.

I'll put flowers
on my husband's grave,
the widow plans,
and later visit
my sister.
She's always glad
of a chat.

Today I retire.
Forty years with the city council
and tomorrow I'll dig
my new garden,
the tram driver smiles.

I'll join my friend
and sit in the shade
under the cherry trees,
chatters the old man.
I'll read
my new poem
aloud to him.
His daughter
will bring us tea.

Six minutes…
we'll dump this thing…
then like we practised
emergency turn
to starboard, full power,
keep turning,
climb like crazy…
get the hell
outta there,
he yells into the intercom,
over the roar of pistons,
the vibrations of air.
Twenty thousand feet
and fifteen miles south
of Hiroshima,
the captain of Enola Gay.

A hundred thousand people
expected to live that day
and no one did.

The wind

I am the wind
and I scatter
nations into sand.

I dissolve the clocks
into fragments,
beats in the moving air.

I sweep away the breathing
and I sweep away the years.
Centuries erode the canyons,
highways decay into fear.

Out on the edge
of dreamlands
foundations built on sand.

Sandhills flow
into cities.
I scour the suburbs
to arid, punish
the boulevards there.

All that remain
are hovels
keening against the air.

Aeons explode
to seconds and the wind
spins away

to the sun.
My sands burn down
to their dreaming.

I am the wind
and my breathing
buries cities there.

Jacarandas in spring

November comes again;
the year rushes to an end.

Outside the study windows
evergreens flourish in the heat
and jacarandas scatter
flower-bursts of colour
across the sky and the lawn –
pools of exotic blue and mauve
swirl against the green
like twilight
or the sea.

Joy in spring, excitement
at the coming of the sun
or lightbursts of horror
like a galaxy of stars,
spinning into purple,
then the violet, then the heat
of a black hole
that bubbles and burns
and from which
nothing returns.

Sunrise: Ile de la Cité

One unhurried sweep and the sky
gathers to pink, frees Notre Dame
from its high, nocturnal disdain
and flings the remnants of the night
to scarlet and reflections in the Seine.

The crusted street stirs to movement,
frees all its coiled springs of commerce –
markets, traffic, taxis in fleets
and the groomed women, prim in pleated skirts,
who glide away on bikes or wait,
neat as statues in the crystal sun.

But down under the old bridge,
shadows from ashen barges cling,
wet and shapeless, to the quay,
and those more furtive, addicted to the night,
still sleep, though some may never wake.

The broad-brush sky selects
stonework into sharp, the arches
and buttresses carved in faces
and sleepy gargoyles who scowl and grimace,
angry at the noise below, where still
in the dark water darker memories flow.

The Rats

after Georg Trakl

A white searchlight moon. Shadows
plummet from the edge of a roof,
silent lives in empty windows
and an easy climb for rats,
hissing, they attack garbage skips or scraps.
Fences shiver in the haze of their dust,
spectral surges of hit and flee,
thick blackened lumps that leap like sprays

of wild bullets. They scramble insanely
over walls and mass in courtyards,
the shock troops of the night's fervent blitzkrieg.
Always autumn's whining, dark, warehouse winds.

Goold Street

Sydney police photographs 1912–1948

A back street in Chippendale,
early 1930s.
A merciless brick wall
intimidates through gloom and height.
Two neat terrace houses
like suspects square the camera.
Some litter
and a battered metal bucket –
spreading stains, spatters of liquid,
dozens of rivulets
pour and pool into precise
perspectives in the nearest gutter.
Almost the corner of Regent Street
never would be close enough
the victim or his crow.
Innocents die, knifed or shot,
so too the less-than-innocent.
The street glowers in black and white,
contrasts brooding light.

Stand at the same corner, face
what the camera faced. Warehouse
windows now bricked in. Weathered walls
demolished and piles of rubble,
rubbish strewn on vacant ground.
Stare down an exposed flank of street.
A February sun batters bricks and walls,
assaults with a spotlit glare.
Sun-blind, stripped of shadows,
this once-was-sinister dark street
slumps in a flash-bulb lens of summer.
Unpainted timbers boarding up
verandas, no wrought-iron tracery
or railings, the houses have become
the slums they were supposed to be –
sadder, derelict and smaller.

The photograph's still eerie with
someone's shadow. A vigil kept in glass,
seventy years votive to a life,
an epitaph that's merely made of light.
Somewhere, someone holds a knife.

Rain at midnight

and the street lamps
turn the asphalt
into velvet.
Halos of light
and glints of silver
where the water
pools in hollows.

Rain flickers
and the tarmac's jostled
into a soft rhythm.
The air melts to a curtain
billowed by raindrops,
folds of light sinuous
with their damp intent.

Every streetlight's
a yellow cone,
an oasis of shimmer
against blackness
that moves.

Newcastle

A hotel balcony, fourth floor,
the mist and grey of waterworld.
Only Stockton's urban sliver
and gravel, metallic, the Dyke
between the Basin and the farthest
hemispheres of ocean, nothing else
but the whole heave of river,
rolling down from far horizons,
jagged green otherwheres of marsh,
wetlands, glass and grey as tabletops,
and water-sheet and loch and mere.

Small hotels confront the river.
A sweep of polder but
like a soft town, cathedral hill
and lowland tongue, all submit
to the long juggernaut of flow.

Colliers, deadweight tens of thousand tonnes
lumber upstream, ride high against the surge.
Atolls of afterworks, lagoons of hatches,
platforms railed on steel, forefoot
muscled against the current by
an aftermath of tugs. They're swung
and berthed to swallow coal.

To fit the flow, bedrock titans
rolling deep, the river channels them
low and drumming downstream now,
away with steel and diesel, coal and water,
to merge with the sweep of flood, they
mesh in the rise of the sea.

Burn

The Milky Way glows
with networks of ice
that link the stars
like highways.
It's two in the morning.
My lounge room hums with heat.
The fire smoulders low.

Skeletons of logs
peck and crackle in the grate,
pop in small explosions
like dust storms on the moon.
Ash showers stir
in tumbles and puffs of charcoal.
A flicker of burnt-out logs,
strings of fire and arteries –
red highways between points of light.

Looking down, thousands of feet
of silent air, the glow
of cities, their faces to the sky
like bright saucers –
a night flight, Sydney to Vienna.

Photographs of Europe burning,
aerial reconnaissance
of patterns woven by infernos,
fire bombings, buildings ablaze, collapse
in firestorms, sirens and searchlights,
roads of asphalt melt
and boil into liquid tar.

I stand in the new railway station
built on the ruins of Dresden
and smell the bodies burn.

Skeletons of firewood collapse
in the grate, stark as teeth,
monuments to the evening's fire,
a hollowed pile, rubble and dust,
I'll sweep away tomorrow.

It's two in the morning.
My lounge room hums with heat
and far above
the cold stars burn
like cities in the sky.

The Pit, the Labyrinth, the Tower

Always the city, always the darkness.
Sunlight on the skin, shadows in the eyes,
darkness between the harbour and the street,
darkness on the street and in the sky.

Ghosts stalk the lacquered hills,
no longer hills, valleys no longer
valleys, suburbs laced with bitumen and brick.
Among the alleyways and lanes,
a spectral city rises to the stars,
built on nothing, towers of glass and mind.

Between the gullies and the cliffs
arcades support the gloom. Traffic moves
across the old headstones, buried now
in Belmore Park. A forest of arches
where sandstone pillars rise between
the tramway and the road. Tunnels drive
through the graveyards of an older city.
On Regent Street the Mortuary Station
builds from the flower beds and lawns.

Something's missing. Something's gone.
The Eora, Dharug, Dharawal,
Kurringai, Gundungurra,
William Dawes and his observatory,
Patyegarang, her tribe, Prince's Street
and Windmill Row.

Barangaroo was once the Hungry Mile.
Day Street shouldered Darling Harbour.
Wooden piers have gone, apartments
ring the harbour now. A tide rises –
new cities of concrete and ghosts.

Inside the Carlton Brewery site
excavators disturb the past,
truckloads of yellow clay, water seeps.
Gravediggers build new arcades
of glass and steel above the Cleveland Swamp,
a labyrinth of lanes and streets. The pit
still underlies the city and its ghosts
still walk between the laneways and the sky.

Commonwealth Street

Walking towards the city,
a different direction
and an unfamiliar street,
the three-way intersection
and a kind of square –
a minor and two major streets
that cross just south of the CBD,
a place I don't remember
ever walking to before.

Gazing, surprised at difference
grown among the ordinary and mundane –
a building seen a thousand times
distant in a known landscape,
now dwarfed by another,
stately, majestic, beautiful,
I'd never known was there.

A few blocks each direction,
familiar views the safe,
familiar streets – not here,
this suddenly exotic place.
The body of an alien city,
its character and breath,
its romance, charm and squalor –
Paris, Barcelona, Rome, Madrid.

An afternoon walk, northern Surry Hills.

A different context –
your friend's face, your lover's smile,
an expression hardly seen,
a body moving in a different way,
a novel phrase or tone of voice,
a changed person,
complete stranger.

Dresden, Copenhagen, Chicago, Leeds.

Lima, Lagos, Brazzaville?

Mosman Bay

The headlands twist
eastward and Robertson Point
almost land locks this thin
suburban backwater.
Apartments, houses, gardens
tumble like a child's
forgotten blocks
and jostle on terraces –
steps and laneways end
where boatsheds
and the bay shimmer.
The Good Friday sun
pours down on yachts
fretting at their moorings
and the wharves advertise
only with their names –
Musgrave Street, Old Cremorne,
Mosman.

A low, insistent throb
regular as heartbeat,
high and angular as a swan,
the ferry threads the bay
and noses towards
this holiday.

Passengers from the city
bring news of politics
and ploys, power, crimes
and crucifixions.

Beyond Curraghbeena Point
the green and yellow Freshwater
slides down harbour
towards Manly.

Miles above
a four-engined jet
with the tail markings
of a foreign country
leaves precise vapour trails
and struggles
to gain altitude
for its flight
across the sea,
across the empire,
across the world.

From the window

An Airbus claws at the rooftops
slowly descending into a chaos
of concrete and brick and steel.
Like a praying mantis,

like a creature from
another history,
another place.
A pterodactyl

or a vast angel
answering a prayer,
powerful, merciless, here.

The exterminating angel.
Every saint and every skyline
generates this fear.

Contentment

In the distance
the slow grumbling of a plane,
ten minutes out of Kingsford Smith,
struggling to gain altitude,
the Sydney–Melbourne flight path,
a few miles north
of where I sit,
my quiet lounge room.

In the bright blue
I've watched their vapour trails
like scarves
wrapped around the sky.

I've sat belted, poised
on the port side of a Boeing
and watched my town slide away
like a smudge on a green carpet
and further to the east
the great, blue Pacific
that seems the edge of the known world,
a border I've slipped across
in dreams and premonitions.

For Christmas I gave you
a blue scarf. You gave me
a green cup, heart shaped –
the male sky, the female earth
exchanged in private mythologies
of love
as if the planet decrees
the small things must
reflect the vast.

Somewhere south of Brisbane
lightning off the starboard wing
and storm clouds deep as cauldrons
that plummet down
to the black heart of the world
as a diver falls through darkness
into the long fathoms,
the plane diverted out
across the coast
like a ship running before the storm,
gathering in the sea miles
merely to escape.

I've struggled through dreams
black as air,
felt lightning on my skin,
and in my lounge room
struggle now to grasp
contentment like a vapour,
soft as the sky
and thunderstorms building
on the horizon.

On Lines by Wallace Stevens

Looking out the window
I see the planets gathering
in the dusk
like leaves turning
in the wind
and night falling
like the eyes
of birds,
like the branches
of skeleton trees
and the cold dresses
of summer girls
who step with delicate,
long legs
across the sky
in the angles
between Jupiter
and my eyes
like moonlit birds
in their filaments of gold
or a child
reciting the alphabet,
who begins at V
and gets to Z
too soon.

Sunset

The wind moves
the summer branches
as if the lord
of terror and suspense
had filmed them silently,
as if the restless trees
wanted to walk
like women in the the sun,
with cotton dresses
and parasols,
who flow
in the movement of a crowd
across a bridge
towards sandhills and the sea,
below a sunset
that is golden,
brilliantly erotic
and intense
as a scream
but fades to darkness
nonetheless.

Acting

for Mary Haire

Slip your arms through new skin,
up over your head –
a moment of panic
in the darkness,
but isn't there always…?

You adjust,
smooth your doubts
down over your stomach,
across your hips,
tight so it presses
the back of your knees

and you move,
not with the gait
you've lived with
but sometimes younger, often older,
and not the gestures
you're used to, but his –

the stranger
who's melted into you,
the ghost who rises from the page
in clouds of ink that vibrate
and paper sprayed
onto your clothes,
new dimension that probe
the silence
that's become you,
that has entered you,
that has your name.

Acting the part

He's there, he's waiting for you,
dressed only in ink, on the flat,
innocent page.

No dimensions but black.
Force your life into him,
wound his anonymity

with your voice and your body,
the intricacies
of a mind alien to his.

Read him into life. Your muscles
raise him into acres of here,
leagues of rise, fathoms of fall.

He's nothing like you but becomes you.
Speak him. Breathe him to talk,
build him on the stage, now

like a monument, the weight of you
under him. Tense his words,
scaffold his arms, carve his face

with your pain, heave him onto
the others. They'll see him only if
you nail him against the lights.

The Spider

On a line by Kristine Ong Muslim

'We are all wolves drunk with stealth.'
The silent pack crossing the plain
between the river and the distant hills
before the hunters and the guns,
before the morning comes.

We are all prowlers sick with dreams.
The midnight alley that terrifies
we walk down anyway.
The shadows that keep moving,
the figure smoking in the doorway.

We are all intruders tense with need.
The empty house we enter not
to steal but just to know what's there.
The closed window that isn't locked,
the door waiting for our knock.

The drives and lusts we only
half acknowledge crawling from the Id,
the universal lattice of the web
that draws towards the small and venomous,
the spider inside every one of us.

On the road, Grenfell to Forbes

Off to the left a light, close, not moving.
A house? Then its gone
but reappears… On the left, a light, close,
not moving. And this goes on
for minutes, for minutes. The dark road,
the scrub, a few trees, small hills,
undulating,
until the car's lights flash
from the oncoming curve, then dim
and you lower your high beam
and pass.

Two cars
bright in the middle of nowhere, fast
between towns…ships at night,
oceans of time to see
and wonder at each other's lights,
if you know it's a ship
or a car, maybe something else.

Change of seasons

Scattered, occasional showers
replace the downpour and the floods
after the summer's frantic heat.
Grey, heat-stained skies like uniforms,
the colour of prisoners and their guards,
mask the shackled sun. Tornadoes
twist and elbowed columns of air,
wield their picks and shovels, drill Kiama.

Skilled, specialist, emergency teams,
trained and paid for by James Hardie, all dead
of lingering lung disease, years ago.
The company's in New York now,
never heard of 'Where is that place?'
where asbestos sheets fragment to dust
clustered by the wind, like thin Chernobyls
swirling in the street.

A climate muscled onto steroids, grass
crackles under feet, azalea bones,
and the creek trickles between ponds,
remnant of rivers, catastrophic fire
predictions, warnings to evacuate
phoned into homes, the carnage of fires.

Broad-arrow damp and iron-gang heat
press their slime against the woodwork, outside
balcony timbers stained to green.
Doors warp with the moisture
and will not close, stench of stagnant water,
stagnant air, stagnant days, all
the threatening overseers of summer,
the convict scowl of cloud banks piled
in their sullen skies. The chain-gang
change of seasons shuffled into autumn.
Humidity's taut like a tarpaulin
lashed to the sodden roof of March.

Discipline and beauty

Saddle 11, a photograph by Helmut Newton

The blackness of a grand piano
merges with its own shadow
thrown against closed double doors.
A tasteful room, Parisian,
an armchair in floral,
its shadow merging with that
of the woman,

who's posed in a saddle, fixed on it
like a rider holding reins,
dressed provocatively, her skirt
hitched up to show a stockinged leg,
long and elegant, a garter,
a flash of bare thigh. Her black jacket
open at the front displays a black bra
and spectacular cleavage.

                Dominatrix…
her hair's severe and disciplined,
her shadow thrusting forward thrown
against the wall but her gaze is fixed
beyond the piano. She ignores the photographer
and listens perhaps to orders
and is anxious to obey. A dominatrix
but still submissive to someone
stronger than herself.

Is it fear on her face or lust to please?
And one detail, a flower, cream or yellow,
on her lapel. It too throws a shadow,
as does the riding crop unnoticed
in the blackness of her skirt,
held tightly in her tightening hand.

Frog Hollow

Where Albion Street
meets Riley – Frog Hollow,
sunk below them both,
a lawn, paths that cross
and ancient steps,
narrow as a laneway
leading down.

And looking up
sandstone walls
that lock you in,
the old escarpment
disguised by the backs of buildings
but not disguised here.

A pleasant park
in Surry Hills
with a long history
as dark as a psychopath
holding a razor
or the shivers of cold rain
hissing down the black windows
of the brothels
across the road.

Paddington Reservoir

Sitting in the shade,
metal chair supplied,
rows of arches like an aqueduct
but the roof's collapsed
from age and rain years ago
and now sunken gardens,
vines and trellises,
staircases that wind down
from the open sky,
from the blast of traffic
to the cool floor
where I'm reading
alone in silence,
in comfort and contemplation
and the memory of what
was once nothing else
but water.

Venus

Morning star and evening star, twin princess
of love, the Chaldeans knew you Ishtar.
You are *nin-si-anna*, Anahita,
Aphrodite, Tai Po and Nin Chien.
The brightest star most glamorous of worlds.
Silver clouds reflect the light, shimmer green
and blue, announce the soft, cool hues of night.
Goddess of romance, sweetest Venus you

spit your vitriol, a hellfire cauldron,
an atmosphere that reeks of sulphur, holocausts
of chlorine, caustic acid, fluorine compounds
seep and pour in virga, acid rain, most
vicious planet of the eight, chemicals
and spitfire venom, beauty, vengeance, hate.

The rain and mud

Thunder stomps among the hills
and humid air descends like rags,
clouds of mere oblivion,
smells of dankness trapped within
leaves and flowers in gutters, drains,
the rank, sweet stench of cardboard mulched
and old lawn cuttings, unwashed clothes.

Silent eyes of children slide
along the lilies and the songs of birds
when in their vortex soft as breath,
waters in their sleep, a tide
of rivers widens into brown,
as thunder loads the sliding hills
with spits and growls, with rain and mud.

Closest to rain

The skin-bone, bare-boned willows pray,
gravestorm their creeks of pleated hair.
Lovemaker turn and see the sky,
great, glacial ships of clouds, spined
filaments of light, snow-skinned
fingerfuls and all your bones made signs.

Icicle spars, ice-veined the tidal air,
sea-relics, sky dragons, shrapnelled messengers
and all their inundation of droplets
are blue hieroglyphs in caves of ice,
sinister the quiet spiders,
their wheels of spinning air.

The river drags a cloak of memory
and ruin, spans of wind.
Sky bodies throw handfuls of the sea
and what makes the water holy is
among the spindled trees
the closest thing to rain.

An old river

This is an old river that loops
in wide meanders and long reaches
past the cities sprawled on its plain, under
bridges and down to oblivious seas.

This is a silent river that has watched
the sins of the past, slow histories of
genocide and spectacles of murder,
knows where the bodies are buried

or left floating headless, has heard
narratives of suicide and rape but
is still beautiful at night when it holds
all its secrets as tightly as the stars.

Wind

The huge nor'wester's
like a locomotive,
roaring down from the distance,
through the tunnel of trees,

its mass
the hammer blow
of pistons, cylinders, its rush
wheels and rods

that hurtle into us,
a juggernaut
of solid, heavy air,
an express train,
moving fast,
flying.

Silence

It's not an absence of noise.
It's heaviness, stillness, strength,
You can feel it
pressing against your eardrums

and you respond to it,
like a swimmer feels the water,
like a diver feels the air,
it's there.

Felling the banksia

Half the old tree was dead.
Its leaves and branches like a skeleton
of finger bones gnarled in the wind,
its trunk thicker than my body.
I doubted our ability and strength
to cut it down.

Three hours it lasted. We
took turns hauling on the handsaw
while the other heaved on the rope
fixed around the main branch
to open up the groove and work
the teeth against its inner wood,
to slide inside the space where steel can gnaw
and even then, many rests to catch our breaths,
as our muscles ached, revolted
against the tedium of push and pull.

At last it fell, branches flailing
for balance against the sky, where once
the big trunk was like a monument
we'd cut away its feet, a diver
without foundation, crushed against the earth.

We whooped and laughed, congratulated
each other and looked at the wreck
with satisfaction, relieved our work
of vast destruction was over.
Now, we thought, the easier job for us
of cutting off the branches
and hauling them away, like debris
from a city, its buildings undermined
while the smaller living trunk, green and fresh,
remained as a portent of the future

as the old trunk might sprout again
with green shoots as cities rise despite
the bombs and the fire and the wind,
as divers swim to the surface, as trees grow.
At least for now we hope so.

At dusk

the sun is below the hills.
Grey clouds gathering in the east
radiate a green light
that seems artificial

but is not.
Each tree glows with a sheen
that is not its own
and the grass is strange.

There is thunder in the distance,
electricity in the air.
The world is an aquarium.
We are looking in. Or out.

Where can we go from here?

And yet

Some dreams become permanent –
a child entering a dark house
or knocking on a door
that no one opens
or a place where something happened
you can't forget,
or where nothing's happened, yet.

Every train

Every train's an uncertainty,
departing here from the present
to a destination
that could be sweet
or could be sour as hurt
or disappointment,
somewhere as huge
as the future
or as tiny as yesterday.

Unveiled

The rain sets in,
cold, thin, insistent drops
and the mist rolls through the valley
like a veil.

The face of the escarpment,
the trees, our neighbour's house and stables,
in a mystery of grey and white,
soften like a bride,

in modesty and grace
floats ethereal and pure,
the long nave of hills and sky.

Until in time the morning comes,
another sky unveiled, naked, clear,
her gorgeous gown unhooked, discarded,
the waiting, carnal, bridegroom sun.

Bombo

for Charmian Clift, who was born here

An empty horizon
strung between headlands,
an empty beach.

A fence beside the tracks.

From the railway
nothing but the sea,
beach and stunted bush.
To the west
four lanes of road
and the graveyard.

We've passed the black teeth
of the quarry, a ravine,
remnants of rock,
sheer and square as ruins.
The train clatters like a pilgrim
onto the viaduct,
crosses the lagoon,
risks the tunnel south.

An explosion of neatness –
houses, shops and parks,
the next valley cluttered
with a coastal toy town,
ornaments arranged to fill a cabinet.

But here there are wolves
on the doorstep, brigands on the porch,
the wilderness beyond the wall,
the town's gate open but guarded.

Water, darkness and then
the wayfarer comes home,
the city, the street, the room.
Of course, every gate's
an exit too.

The roads and railway
also lead
away.

Baby, can you hear me?

Baby, can you hear me now?
The chains are locked and tied around my door.
Baby, sing with me somehow

                                            Neil Young

I'm alive to a world of words,
those that I sing to you,
those that flame on my screen,
stripped direct from your fingers –
the keyboard alphabet of blooms,
your blood-red nails I hold
like keys in the broken locks
of the chains around my heart,
your voice in my rhymes and verse.

There's a part of you that pours from me
in lines like wine on my tongue,
the blood of your lipstick in my mouth,
eyeliner black as the angels' robes –
choirs who chant their hymns like flowers,
the images and words reflected back to you
that pour from me in chords
I take entirely from you.

Small violets ripple across the lawn
like syllables, this early spring.
I'm scared
of purple worlds, the windswept words
of angels and their dark unfolding wings
raised in the wind like doors.
I'm scared of their words and their song.
Baby, I love you because
you're never scared for long.

Erotic Poems

I watched her there, between me and the moon…
                                            Theodore Roethke

I never wrote erotic poems for you,
dark angel, till you showed me all
that intricate geometry lies hidden in
your skin and heart and bone.
Now I compose you into darkened flame,
the flower that bursts from shadows,
your silver petals bloodied by the moon –
my moon encompassed in your bracelet arms.

I write you to a point of fire, dazzled
in the pain of light I touch your eyes
in trees and stone, your breath dissolves
in themes of night, in poems from stars.
I capture you in words, this verse for you
to kill the emptiness between the moon and you.

Andromeda

Between the table and your lip,
in the glass you lift to your mouth,
ride on your indrawn breath.
I am the prince of foxes.

From here to Andromeda
take the foxtail air,
swallow galaxies and spin red ribbons
around your red tattoo, the moons

of pearls and your fragrant neck.
The stem of your glass, a cool gaze
of lipstick, red as the comet's kiss
you breathe to the firefox dancing.

Nowra, evening

All afternoon the town's
been drilled by sunlight.
The evening brings a cooling
and a softening of buildings.

The easterly erodes angles,
the insane blaze, the frantic sun
and the white, screeching air
where only dazed corellas shriek,
excited to be still alive
in trees that stand as leaves and branches,
not as sun-blind caverns
blackened by the glare.

Walls have become domestic
with comfort and shadow, variety
in differences of woodwork, of cream
and beige, the exactitude of bricks.
It's possible to walk and keep thinking.

The cloudless, more humble sky's
available now in tints of blue and shade.
The streets and shopfronts delivered safely
from annihilation by heat and sun
offer a precision of detail,
waiting for appraisal
in the tender light.
The town relaxes into life.

A black dress

Your dress
is the darkness of the night.

Sensual astronomers know
stars are only born
and burn and then they swell
and burst with such intensity
they leave only ash-grit, brittle rings,
so brilliant, so fleeting
in the immense, eternal plenitudes
of space. So profound the night
their light becomes the merest glimmer,
shallow as wings.

Your dress
is the darkness of the night.

You stand there glamorous,
darkling, beautiful
so the transience of light
burns itself to ashes
nightly in your sight.

Here to far

for Gabriella and Silvana Mangano

From here to far the wind
boils in the ribboned air,
throws tentacles and claws
among the grass which bends
under its pelt and sweep,
while the trees flow
like abandoned boats unmoored
by rivers that surge and run.

Two sisters, their movement's rhyme
and rhythm, swirling skirts,
identical in simple black –
a ball of ribbon thrown
each to each in time
to all that cascades in the wind
like a cat, like love, like a poem
unfolding in their arms.

Again and again

The golden desk lamp,
the green shade, the night
again and then again
the blank page waiting

and the darkness in my mind,
my fingers itching to write,
searching the light of the lamp.
the green shade, the night.

Signals

The western tracks tangled into Redfern,
complexity in the rows of six-light,
automatic signals, dazzling
the rain, piercing the steel-bright mist –
the Up Main, the Up Suburban
and on the Up Local, wormlike, a train
threads the points through Eveleigh,
the Illawarra Dive, gantries
and the overhead, this portal
to the city and into Central Yard.
The clarity of red on red –
Stop! The green and the red. Caution!
The orange, the double green on green.

Out of the gloom ahead, the green clears
to pass, then flicks to hazard after us.
Do not pass here! Our train's guarded
in this section by the locked-down
double red, the press and loom of danger.

On the other track the orange and the green.
Your section's clear and the next, but slow down,
an eight-car Interurban's now two sections
ahead of you. And then the red on green.
This section may be clear to pass
but the next is not – all you'll see is stop.

It's early, a grey morning, late in spring.
No crowds, the trains and tracks are quiet
and you're travelling to another future,
railways devour time. Ride on from here,
but not this future, not this life.
You'll never get such signals, clear, precise.
No judgement marks the road ahead with lights.
No future's ever exact like this.

Don't frighten me

after Anna Akhmatova

Don't frighten me with threats of hollowness and loss,
the ice-blow thought of life separate from you.
For me, another short absence, that's all.
For you just another journey away.

It's true we've never greeted the dawn together
or watched the moon gliding above the roof
so today I offer you gifts unheard of before:
our reflections in the mirror; submission
before the tears of midnight and the fantasy of sleep;
a glance that only you can decipher
to guide you into the orbit of my dreams;
an echo of our laughter within that room;
our voices from the past and our voices now
so you can listen without shudder or guilt
to the gossip of crows, the cries of hawks,
so the memory of sleet and wind in the winter night
becomes sweeter than breezes tender with the spring.

Remember me, my dark and distant angel,
remember me, at least until the winter and the winds.

Knocking

But you stand there so nice
in your blizzard of ice –
Oh, please let me come into the storm.
Leonard Cohen

After the storm
and its theatricals –
the bombastic thunder,
the fey lightning,
comes the rain
like a knocking.

I see you, bold ingenue,
clean, immaculate, integral
like a bird of the night,
your skirt damp with moonlight,
your hair silver with rain.

The morning
makes her quiet entrance
almost unnoticed,
bound like a thief,
lissom and pale
as a ghost –
like a question.

I cannot find the answer.
I cannot hear the question
above the rain.

The transaction

Early winter, thirty years ago,
the first home I'd ever owned.
Every afternoon downstairs to water
the sapling near the balcony…

And now it's June and once again
our warm apartment and its lower sun
shadows into dark and grim.
The thirty-metre adult tree
begins the annual month-long rite
of browning down, strips away
its lace-green gown and summer skirt
and naked like a dryad stands
to welcome in the sun.

But no transaction's ever fully fair.
For weeks our balconies and pot plants,
carpets, floor and drying clothes all fill
with ground-down, fine-minced mulch of leaves.

For a little water years ago
the tree insinuates its breath
between the window and the sill,
among the mornings and our dreams
so all its compost spreads
that in exchange for warmth and light
the great green cycles come
of life and growth and death.

Delphi

Stand on Omphalos,
navel of the world.
Here the Phaistos valley
dizzies down to amphitheatres
of stone and air and space. The mind
empties to a canyon –
a staircase for giants
and the drama of dreams,
brief comedies of birth and life,
tragedies of age and death,
hewn in rock and acted here
on the earth's central stage
and in the world below
with the huge silence of years.

The foot of Mount Parnassus,
a step of almost level ground,
remnants of the temple
to Apollo, ruined god
of the ruined sun.

On this ridge, cliff and air alone,
three Doric columns like a sign,
the remains of rock
built on rock, raised
in the arms of the world
that hang above the world.

The Sybil's rock, daughter
to the mysteries of then and now
and the mysteries of the future –
the great hollowness of years to come.
The priestess plunges down
through creation's mind and myth
to where the belly of the earth
still sings to us in oracles
that riddle our lives like truth.

The magic city

Pedestrian bridges
that arch like cats
and bright buildings
to guide the dark river
into the heart
of the afternoon.

The length of the yellow station,
red bricks and sunset
flashing from the windows
of crystal towers.

Wanderers and crowds
on the boulevards,
palaces and spires
above the black of older
domes and turrets.

The masts and shrouds
of a three-masted barque
from the diamond century
and the stone facade of the cathedral
and modern trams
that bustle
like slow mice
across the dark river
into the heart
of the magic city.

Opening night

Frederickton, Nova Scotia, 11 May 2008

'First we take Frederickton, then we take Berlin!'

A clip-on sign outside a theatre:
Monday – The Babington Brass Band.
Tuesday – Leonard Cohen. Wednesday –
Silvershoes, Elvis Impersonator.
Fifteen years since he'd stood
anywhere near a stage, five years
a Zen Buddhist monk –
'I've had it with the music racket,'
at 74, 'just a kid
with a crazy dream,' Leonard Cohen
was singing again.

Rat-pack rabbi, suits and hats,
a six-piece band, three backing singers,
no one knew what to expect
but Leonard Cohen was singing again.

Like a supplicant, head held low
like a prayer, whispers the intimate,
his life in song, intricate
the secrets of the self-aware,
ironic, honest, the journey for the beauty –
they all came.
Drop your voice from your throat
to your heart
and sing again.

It's got to inject perfection.
Don't forfeit the people's time
with anything less, don't
betray your art, no public
prostitution with a bauble
in a song.

But what if I can't?

What if no one wants to hear me?

The theatre held seven hundred,
they could have sold that night
ten times those tickets
and in the months, the years
to come, one hundred times
but here was the beginning:

'Dance me to your beauty
like a burning violin…'

They went wild.

Women cried.

When your email came

Your email came.
I was walking on air.
This vertical world's
an achieved fantasy,
an in-drawing of breath.

Walking on air's
a thin footfall,
soft as nothing
between the syllables
of your longest kiss.

When gravity's collapsing,
energy's exploding
into force fields of space,
stride on the lonely sun
sprawled below my soles
and then I'm
breathing clouds.

No muscles, no shoes.
Just a huge uplifting Yes!
Every angel's seen
and your sweet words
are huge
across the sky's vast
electric, virtual screen.

www.ingramcontent.com/pod-product-compliance
Lightning Source LLC
Chambersburg PA
CBHW062149100526
44589CB00014B/1755